Your Fellow Empath

Kenzie Chapman

Published by Kenzie Chapman
Interior design by Rebecca from SelfPubMagic

Library of Congress Control Number:
2024924089

Hardback ISBN: 979-8-9911761-1-8
Paperback ISBN: 979-8-9911761-0-1
E-book ISBN: 979-8-9911761-2-5

First Edition Print 2024

To the ones that feel
too much

Contents

Foreword

I was always told I got the empath gene from my mom. Does it make me much different from the next person? No. But there is something so liberating, and also heartbreaking about being someone who feels everything. I want this collection of poems to transfer into what I felt at the time. Peaceful, scared, happy, sad, hopeless, hopeful, believing in nothing and believing in everything. Us humans are very complex and very contradictory. We want to rebel and we want to follow the rules. There is a yin and yang aspect to every human, I think. The way I wrote these poems was at random. Random times, random days, days that I felt everything and days that I felt nothing at all. So I chose not to create themes. Because humans don't control the themes of life, I want this collection of poems to simply be, a collection of poems. We don't choose when we get heartbroken, or when we lose a loved one or a friend. We don't choose when we fall in love, it just happens. Some of our most amazing moments come on days unexpected. So as you flip through each new page, I want the theme of the poem you're reading to be unexpected. Each day brings new opportunities, and each page of my book brings a drastically different perspective. So for now, I hope you enjoy reading this as much as I enjoyed the process of creating it. Welcome to Your Fellow Empath.

create > consume.

Childhood wounds
Of feeling insignificant.
Of feeling like you can't
Explore your curiosity.
Of being bad
Before even realizing
What bad means.
Curiosity being
An innocent way
Of exploring
What life means.
Childhood wounds
Taken into adulthood,
Tainting genuine
connections,
These wounds
Causing
Now adults
To question their
Own intuition.
Like, seriously
What will happen
To me if I sin?
Condemned to hell,
But isn't that the
Words I hear from
The religious?
But what about
Each Sunday in church
When they talk about
Forgiveness?

->

This isn't the way it's
supposed
To be.
I'm supposed
To explore my curiosity
Freely.
I'm supposed to learn
For myself.
This controlled environment
Ends up
Suffocating me,
And pushing me,
Further and further
Toward even more chaos.
Why can't everyone
Realize that everyone
Is trying to do what's right?
And what's right
Looks different
For each set of eyes.
Our struggles could
Unify us,
But instead
Our judgment
Ends up
Ostracizing
Everything
And everyone.
If we could live
In a world
Filled with more
Shameless curiosity,
Imagine how much
Lower the crime rates
Would be.

I'm a truth seeker.
I want to make mistakes.
I don't want to live
Within the confines of
Other's perspectives.
I want to lead
By my own intuition.
And realize
That my soul's mission
Was made
To explore,
To Transmute,
To Suffer,
To want more.
My soul knew
My journey
Here on this earth.
So let me
See what I'm worth.
I am not defined
By my downfalls.
I am defined by
My wanting to
Be more.
More kind,
More selfless,
More understanding,
More me.

your fellow empath

Self respect can be so hard
When you want them
Just one more time.
One more kiss,
One more hug,
One more
I love you.
But sadly,
The way they are treating you
Has no reflection of loving you.
Their actions say,
"I want nothing to do with you."
Their actions say, "you're just a pass time.
Let me have you
When I'm lonely
Or sad,
Or wanting someone
In my bed."
Their words say, "I love you!
Keep me around!"
But their actions say,
"I don't care
If I lose you,
Someone better
Can be found."
And when you finally leave
Out of self respect,
They'll come begging
For you back.
Taking accountability
And promising that
The cycle won't keep
Repeating.
When in their head
They knew all along,
They were a liar.
Purposefully deceiving.

And unfortunately,
You believed them.

Stop.
Just stop.
Please.
Just fucking stop.
Stop caring,
Stop feeling,
Stop crying,
Why can't you stop?
Why so sensitive?
So fearful?
So anxious?
So bitter?
So pessimistic?
Angry even!!!
Oh
I see.
You're hurt.
And hurt people
Either feel everything,
Or nothing
At all.
Maybe both?
One day hot,
One day cold.
But nothing?
Nothing being
An expression
Of suppression.
And everything?
Everything being
A feeling of
Unfortunate proof.
Unfortunate proof
Of chaos
And lies.

->

But wait,
Please
listen.

Don't lose yourself
In this depression!
Can you do this one
Thing for me?
Don't stop feeling.
Because you're only human.
Don't lose your humanity
In the injustices
Served to you,
By people
Just like you and me.
We're all the same.
We're all hurt.
And we have no want
Of hurting ourselves
Or others more.
So please,
Let your emotions flow.
Heal them,
Feel them,
Sit through them,
Grieve them.

This,
This is the natural state
Of being human.

Why did I let you in?
Now I'm the one that
Feels broken.
You're excuses
Are sickening,
I'm sick of
Your cop outs.
"You didn't give me what I needed."
"A man has needs!"
Well fuck you.
Cause you already
Fucked me
Emotionally,
Mentally,
Spiritually.
So tell me?
What makes you think
I'd give in physically?

-boys in the 21st century

I feel like I can't get up.
The grief is so overwhelming.
Grieving those I lost,
Whether
From trauma
Or disrespect
Or death.
Sounds morbid
I know,
But that's the reality
Of it all.
Grief is horrible.
It changes you
On a fundamental level.
Sometimes
I just want to pick
Up the phone and dial.
To talk about anything
And everything.
To hear your voice.
But in the couple of seconds
Between picking up the phone
And dialing,
The realization kicks in.
It rushes in
So unexpected.
The realization that
I can't talk to you
Ever again.
Because,
Well,

You won't be on the other end
Of the line.

Suppression of the soul,
It's an overwhelming
And vast
Hole.
Dark and dreary,
Treacherous and depleting.
Suppression of the soul.
But just imagine
For a second,
That it's opposite day.
Let's
Reverse
This.
Expression of the soul,
It makes us feel whole.
How funny is it,
That two words
Of drastically different meanings,
Land on our ears
With the same hearing?
How contradicting!
Is it a coincidence?
I don't know.
But hold on.
What does expression
And suppression look like to you?
What are you holding onto?
Why?
What are you not allowing yourself to express?
You know in my understanding
The root of our problems,
Are in the problems themselves.
What do I mean by that?

->

Well
What is
The opposite of the problem
You're facing?
And what barriers,
Insecurities,
Or wounds
Are holding you back,
From fully expressing the you
Who doesn't experience lack?
Who doesn't experience
This so called
Void?

Just,
Think about it.

Someone else's
Talent,
Beauty,
Wealth,
Kindness,
Passion,
Integrity,
Intelligence,
Does not take away
From yours.
We live in an abundant Universe.
And we are all multifaceted,
Loving beings.
With souls of wanted expansion.
Love and acceptance,
More than anything
Else.
Trust that.
The ones that
Have taken the time
To heal themselves
Will see you
For who you are at your core.

And people that have
Healed themselves,

Don't envy others,
They get inspired.

There is beauty
In simplicity.
So much beauty.
In a world
Of so much complexity
How can I choose
To remain
True to me?
It's simple.
Simplify,
Rectify,
Feel it out,
Let it die.
Then go back,
Back to what you
Do best.
The basics,
The fundamentals.

The beauty of
Simplicity.

Be careful.
Someone's miracle may
Be something
You take for granted.

your fellow empath

The dark side of girlhood is this.
It's late night conversations
Of slowly admitting "me too."
It's being hated by men
And women for reasons unknown.
It's feeling paranoid and unsafe
Every moment you're alone.
It's old men and relatives
Making cruel and perverted comments
About your body.
It's people thinking they have a say
Over what you should do with your body.
It's she's too confident,
She's not confident enough,
Why is she trying so hard?
She must be insecure,
She's such a sl*t,
She's too innocent,
She shouldn't make that much money.
She should have a job,
She's so selfish!
She should solely be
A stay at home mom.
It's her second guessing,
Meeting new men and
Fearing their true intentions.
It's questioning the motives of
"Boy best friends."
It's boys will be boys,
It's editing how you dress,
And act in order to not
Tempt men.

Girlhood isn't all just
Ease and comfort and joy,
Girlhood shouldn't have a dark side.

The morning light seems to hold
New opportunities that I have needed
For as long as I can remember.
The golden rays shine through
The tinted,
Weathered windows,
Letting me believe in
A better today.

I hope I will not miss the golden
Light on my face for
Yesterday's lonely hours of
Despair and disbelief in
A better tomorrow.

We hold memories and past experiences
As our identities.
But if yesterday
Is gone and tomorrow is
Unknown,
Why do we decide
To hold ourselves to
Everybody else's expectations
Of who they think we are?

A broken mind.
A broken home.
My broken hope.
All that is broken,
Is broke open
So we can see inside and realize,
That we had to shatter to survive.
That we lived in discomfort and agony
In order to mend our broken minds.
Our broken homes.
Our broken hope.
We had to break open to build something new,
To mend our wounds.
To create something we never imagined possible.
Something that had to end in order to begin again.
And when all is said and over,
We can't imagine a better way
That it could have gone over.
In the end it was worth it.
Mended mind.
Happy home.
Restored hope.

Expectations and measurements.
They cramp your style.
They insist that we are only
Valuable by the numbers
or words on
A sheet of paper.
But you,
My friend.
You're so much more than that.
There's proof of that in
Every aspect of life.
Just take a moment to look around.
There is your proof.
Everything we see created in nature,
Created us too.
Yet we still believe that we aren't enough.
That we aren't smart,
Beautiful,
Funny,
capable.
Just tell me why,
In a world full of so much knowledge,
Tell me why
We are still basing our importance
And value on the numbers or words
On a sheet of paper?

There is something about an
Evergreen tree.
Not only is it beautiful,
But it resists the
Coldest and darkest of winters.

I see my life looking in
As if I have no control.
Others make my toils seem achingly effortless.
So why is it that everything seems to be a challenge?
Why is it that,
Well,
I don't know.
And that's just it.
Everything I thought I knew before doesn't seem
To make sense anymore.
How do I move forward when
I feel that my state of affairs will never emit to more?
Why is it that not so long ago
I could control the things that I can't control,
Now?
My mind is telling me one thing,
But my emotions contradict logic saying,
What is the point if I have no hope of
Ever getting better?

Sadness and despair
make the most impactful stories.
Memories.
Art.
Influence.
Connection.
Relatability.
Compassion.
Hope.
Take a moment to believe that
Your story can be all of those things.
Even when you are
Right in the middle of it all.
Take that moment
To surrender to your
Current reality.
Your story is one that
Someone will want to hear.
Just hold on a little longer,
You'll see.

Stop ignoring the real you.
Life's greatest moments
Happen when you take action
In what is genuine to you,
And only you.
Will it sometimes be terrifying?
Most likely.
But will you care once you've
Achieved what you came here to do?
I doubt it.

Nothing in life is too great an issue to
Ignore the sounds of a songbird.
Or the whisperings of the trees,
The giggles or smile of a child,
The music of nature.

The simple pleasures and joys of life.
No grief or pain is large enough.

I've noticed the truth in
Realizing that less is more,
And not knowing may be better.
It used to confuse me,
But then I grew up.
And I realized that
My imagination
Was far more interesting
And innocent.

Growing up is hard.

You were my
Breath of fresh air.
So once I lost you,
I had to become that for myself.
That air became so much
Sweeter once I realized
I had been breathing
For myself all along.
So I'd like to thank you
For our time.
Because of you,
I learned to
Be with me.
And to enjoy
The sweetest
Most wonderful
Moments with the one who
I'll be with for the rest of my life.

Me.
<3

Pain truly tests one's character.
I've seen it firsthand.
Because I was the one
Who's character was being tested.
And like many,
I've fallen short at times.
But that's ok.

For now here is this reminder.
The next time
Someone lashes out at you,
Please just stop to
Question their motives.
How one acts truly is
Just a reflection
Of how they feel inside.

Pain is transferred
If not transmuted,
And it takes time
To learn that.

Am I escaping?
Or am I dreaming?
I prefer the latter.

When I refuse to create
It's no wonder
My head feels as though
It will explode.
Thoughts are
So intrusive,
So deep seeded.
What a muse,
And what a thin line between mad
And brilliant.

What if we were all just
Brilliant?

I never understood how powerful
Just one look could be until
I met you.
You pierced my heart and soul
Within seconds.
I never understood it,
And now I crave that.
I feel so out of control
And I hate It because
I've been in control
For so long.
Years of work to
Be in control,
And you disarmed all of it
Within
A single,
Look.

•your fellow empath

What if we believed
In ourselves
Like we believe in others?

I romanticize falling in love,
But when the opportunity
Comes knocking
At my door,
I slam it shut
And run to hide.

I realized I needed people.
I didn't want to admit it
But now I know for certain,
I need you.

Where's that version of me
That woke up every morning
Excited?
Where is she?
She let her dreams run wild
And chased after them
Every.
Single.
Day.
And now I wake up
And don't feel like her anymore.
Why?

Perhaps the worst
Part of grieving over
How powerless life makes us feel,
Is being unable to define
Exactly what it is that is making
Us feel so disempowered.
Give me the word,
Give me the situation,
Give me an explanation,
For why I feel so extremely empty?
I had an explanation in the past
But now I feel numb to every
Explanation,
And I have no fucking clue where to
Begin.

This is a cry for help.
I need help.
And I am terrified this
Feeling will never go away.

"Try again tomorrow!"

This reality is too painful.

Maybe I'll just go back to sleep.

I seek validation,
But not in the ways you would
Assume.
I seek validation from myself.
A classic mistake
Of a perfectionist.
Someone teach me how
To believe in myself
Without thinking I have to
Do everything perfectly.
At least I am learning,
And that takes time.

Because everything is a process,
I am learning to slow down.
Everything in life is gradual.
Us humans
Overcomplicate
And create issues.
Problems to be solved,
But no realization
That we are right in the
Middle of solving.
Solving takes time.
Solving tests one's patience.
Solving is supplemental.
Reaching the solution
Will come,
But patience in between
The question
And the solution,
Is everything.

Resistance is a funny thing.
There can be a number
Of infinite reasons
Why we resist
Doing what we love,
Following our dreams,
Subconscious beliefs that hold us
Back.
There can be a number of reasons.
But once you push through
And actually do,
Instead of worry,
The breakthrough is worth
Its weight in gold.
Once you break through
That resistance,
You feel as though you
Can do anything.
And you are met
With clarity on the
Other side.
So please,
Don't stay on this side of doubt.
Push through.
Because the grass truly is greener
On the other side
Of what
You've been avoiding.

Have faith in the process.
Have goals,
With no expectations.
It's not what we want to hear,
But it makes the surprise
Of what we wanted to come true,
So worth all the suffering it took
To get there.

Trials in life are expected,
And we are given the tools
To get through them
If we truly believe we can.
But the trial of heartbreak
Is something I wasn't prepared for.
Trials in general
Are met with ways of
Problem solving and coping.
But heartbreak,
It has me questioning everything
I've ever been,
Ever seen,
Ever believed.
It has me questioning myself
And my own motives.
Grieving a person
Is far more painful.
You are not only grieving
A specific person,
You are grieving
Your hopes for a future with them.
The way they laugh,
The way they smell,
The way they hold you,
The way they make
Everything feel better.
Their promises,
Their everything.
It is so heartbreaking
When you realize you
Have to imagine
A future that felt so right with them,
Without them.
I think that's one of the hardest
Things a human can go through.
Goodbye for now,
Or maybe forever.
I guess
It's time for me to
Heal.

Tell me why
My vulnerability
Is such a strength?

Tell me why
How deeply I feel,
Is such a strength?

And if it's such a strength,
Then why do I feel
So weak?

You were never inherently bad.
Nobody starts out that way.
Why do you self analyze
Your every move
And wonder if your choices
Are "bad?"
Why can't you just trust that
You are human?
Why can't you just
Shut your brain off?
Why can't you tell the you,
That started out on this earth,
At the peak of her innocence,
That she was never bad?
And that she never will be?
As long as she keeps trying.

Why don't you realize
That you are digging yourself a
Hole?
And in the midst of digging
This "hole,"
You are searching for what makes
You whole.
Where is it?
Where is God?
Where is healing?
Where is that breath of fresh air?
Please tell me.

I feel like I'm suffocating
Under my own self deprecating
Thoughts.

"She's just looking for attention."
"They're such attention seekers."

What if you read that again
And replaced the word
Attention,
For love?

How hard can it be?
More like,
I'm terrified that if I fail
I'll have to remain like this
Forever.

I don't want to be
Trapped in a constant
Power struggle between
My traumatized self,
And my self
That has always
Seen higher.

your fellow empath

My fear of the unknown
Is affecting my mental health again.

Where did my sense of gratitude go?
Why is it so hard to feel?

Why is pain so easy to keep,
And healing so hard to maintain?

The fish would probably
Rather swim with the current too.

Passion.
What a magical thing,
And what an honor
To experience
Someone in their
Natural state of flow.
Enjoying what they love
And enjoying
What helps them
Make sense
Of this world.

your fellow empath

You know,
Trying to reverse the
Damage that you didn't cause
Is on a whole other
Plane of difficulty.
Controlling
What you can control,
When in the back of your mind
If they just said sorry
And showed it,
The damage might be repairable.
But it's always
The ones
That aren't open
To doing the healing
That cause
The most destruction.

What a vicious cycle.

I realized I needed people.
I didn't want to admit it,
But now I know for certain,
I need you.

your fellow empath

You look at me as if I have
Solved all of your problems,
And been the source of all
Your joys.
You look at me as if
I could end all the pain in this world.
Like I am the most incredible
Sight you have ever seen.
I didn't know how to react to that.
It left me speechless.
And now I am left sitting here
Wondering,
But knowing,

You'll never look at me
That way again.

He saw me like no one ever has.
So why in a world like this,
Did me expressing
How I feel,
Ruin what we had?
If so,
I naturally feel guilt for
Telling the truth.
How sad is that?
I hope my telling him
How I feel for him
Didn't kill
What we have,
Or had for that matter.

-from friends to almost lovers and back to strangers

your fellow empath

I miss everything about you.

Did you ever feel the way that I do?
Or was it all just imaginary?
Was it all just me?

I can't imagine my life without you.
But here I am,
Turning my imagination
Into a reality.

And there's nothing I can do
To change that.

How can I keep blaming every
external situation on my
Internal state of mind?
Aren't I stronger than that?
Aren't I strong enough to
Change how I think?
It feels way too exhausting
Lately.
I'm just so tired.
I'm usually one to think
Optimistically,
But maybe the world finally
Showed me
How cruel it can be
Enough times that I finally
Stopped believing.
I stopped believing they would
Stay.
I stopped believing in the magic.
I tried not to,
And it's been a hard fight.
But man,
It's a hard fight.
I feel imprisoned in my own
Mind with
No plausible tactics
Or forms
Of escape.

Physical pain turns into
Mental and emotional pain,
And mental and emotional pain
Turns into physical pain.

I'm listening to Falling in Love
By Cigarettes After Sex.
But listening to that song
Is so contradictory,
Because I'm not falling in love,
My heart is breaking.

I'm attracting mirrors
All around.
That show up as people,
Whom I feel bound.
I'm not bound
To these people,
I'm addicted
To my own
Procrastination,
Of not breaking through
To the me,
That will find those
To grow with me.
How can I expect
Consistency
When I don't hold
The same energy,
Within myself?
So until
I breakthrough,
I'll repeat this cycle.

The Universe's
Loving way
Of showing me
I'm
Worthwhile.

I crave intimacy.
Today's society,
So animalistic.
We take something so pure
And we pervert it.
A gift from God,
The Universe,
The preference is yours.
Something so natural,
And innocent,
Yet so taken out of context.
It's called dirty and unclean,
"You're sinning!"
"You're too naive!"
Why can't we see that
No one wants that anymore?
The purity of it all.
To be completely truthful,
I think we're all a little scared
Of showing the most
Innocent side of ourselves.
We're too worried
That if we're too real or
Too vulnerable,
Maybe they'll get bored.
Or feel the need to explore.
On to the next right?
Who's better?
Who's brighter?
More beautiful?
But you can't
Stop to look
At what's right in front of you.
We need to stop
Craving emotional
And physical
Intimacy
By masking it,
And calling it
Casual sex.

Our spirits think
We're soulmates,
But our minds
Are are at a stalemate.
My mind fights me,
But my soul
Ignites,
Wanting to do right by me.
My soul knows you,
It knows it wants you,
It knows we could be two
Peas in a pod.
I know it sounds cheesy,
But I think being with you
Would be easy.
Why fight our minds so much?
Are you not empowered
By my touch?
Do you not feel what I feel?
Cause I could've sworn this was
Real.
I could push through the
Blockages
And insecurities
To get to you,
But could you do that too?
I think we're worth the risk,
But it takes two to tango,
And you're not really one to dance.
Are you?
So I guess on our way we go,
Separately,
But still together
In the 5D.

Maybe someday
You'll want to experience
Another realm with me.

Pretty privilege.
Something that is looked at
As a joke.
It's funny and
Super fun,
Until
Men you don't want
To entertain
Won't take no for an answer.
And every excuse or lie you make
Of
"I don't swing that way!"
Or
"My boyfriend is on his way!"
Doesn't matter.
They can't take no for an answer.
And now you're scared
To upset them,
Cause you
don't know
Whether or not
They have a temper.

I’ve never connected with someone
Like I connected with you.
And that's what made it hurt
So deeply.
And now I’m left here wondering
If our connection is still current.
I don’t want you to be the boy
From my past.
I want you to be the man
In my future.

Do it yourself.
Something I always
Thought was necessary.
Because how dare I ask for help?
But tell me,
Why I feel as though
I have to do everything?
Tell me why
I thought
That asking for
Help meant that
I must be weak?
Or incapable?
Or too scared?
Where does that fear stem from
And why do I care?
When in my early years
Was I so hurt
That I resorted to
Doing everything myself?
I think doing everything
Myself
Was easier than asking for help.
Maybe I just wanted
To avoid the hurt of
Being disappointed
And let down,
Every time I asked.

Thank you for showing me
What it's like to be unconditionally
Loved and cared for.
Thank you for making me
Feel seen and heard.
Thank you for making
Me feel at home and
At peace in your presence.
I truly care for you.
I just hope our story hasn't ended.
I hope I get to not just start falling,
I hope we get to finish
What we started.
I hope we can finish
The natural trajectory of
Falling for each other.

your fellow empath

You are just like the boys I read
about in books.
I didn't think you existed,
But you do.
You're everything I could ever want
And more.
So tell me,
Why you're suddenly
Slipping away from my reality?

I didn't think you'd become
Fictional too.

If I get the chance to fall for you
All over again,
It will be worth it.
All the bad,
All the pain
And the heartache,
Will be worth it.
I just want you.
I was sure about you.
But you
Weren't sure about me.
And that genuinely
Kills me.

your fellow empath

You don't make any sense. You're selfish and unfair.
But I knew what you were so why did we go there?
A new experience,
It was fun while it lasted.
But something about not being with you
Makes me feel homesick.
Am I just lonely? Yes and no.
But how can you reject a connection
That helps both of us grow?
Is it one sided?
No. You say you feel the same way,
So I'm confused, why can't we try this?
Why did I let you in?
When at the time you
Came knocking,
I wasn't even ready to comprehend,
Caring like that again?
Too broken from my last but I can't help myself,
I don't want this to be a regret from my past.
So I wore my heart on my sleeve,
Yet again,
And yet again I'm attached.
It's terrifying, but what's even more terrifying,
Is not risking it.
Because now I know I will never be the one
On my deathbed crying,
Wondering,
Reminiscing,
Or grieving
Over the
Heart wrenching
Question of
What if?

I hope our paths cross in the future
When we are both a little more
healed.
Not all the way,
Cause that is impossible
But enough for us to realize,
We needed each other all along.
But then I think about the fact
That we are never healed enough.
I was never healed enough.
But I was willing to do this with you.
Unhealed,
Triggered,
Scared,
And I think I'm ignoring the truth
That is right in front of my face.
You didn't want me enough
To face your
Unhealed,
Triggered,
And scared
Self.

your fellow empath

Your defense mechanism
To not care about me
By avoiding me,
Is hurting me.
Stop leading me on
Cause the cake I gave you
To have and eat too
Is so far gone.
I was your favorite flavor,
I'm something you dreamt about
And savored.
Heaven help me
If I ever decide to give you
Just one more piece.
You don't deserve this sweetness.
Your cake
That you offer
Is gross,
And expired,
And filled with empty promises.
Go bake a new cake,
And come back when it's warm,

Just don't be surprised
When you realize
I like
Brownies more.

You don't know what you have
When you have it.
You search for greener grass,
But realize later,
The grass was always greener
Where you watered it.
You keep trying
To fill the emptiness
Till you find the
"Perfect fit"
Just to find nothing.
Now you're the one alone.
But then you see her,
The one you had,
But left for these
So called
"Greener pastures."
And she looks so abundant,
And whole,
And radiant.
Cause instead of finding
Someone "better,"
She poured all
The water she let flow into you,
Back into herself.

->

your fellow empath

One of the most painful
Karmic lessons of all,
Watching the girl you loved
Receiving everything you wanted
With her
and more.
But you watch
From the outside,
Observing.
And I hope you heal
Cause God knows
The pain that you caused her.
It made her better.
And the pain of seeing her,
Missing her,
Wanting to be with her,
Is far greater.
So you sit and watch
From the sidelines.
Wondering,

"Why didn't I see her
When I had her?
Why did I think
There would be
A greener pasture?"

We really do have a lot to learn
from children.
The older I get,
The more I come to this realization.
From the way they are,
So effortlessly present,
To the way they so freely express
Their emotions.
Good and bad,
Social anxiety almost never exists
In their world.
They see someone with a pretty
Shirt,
Or a cool toy and they say,
"Hey, wanna be my friend?"
Unfortunately,
Growing up in this world,
We're molded
and caged,
Into suppressed versions of our
Inner child.
"I want more friends, but I'm scared
To go up to that person.
What will they think of me?
I'm scared to share my passions,
What if they judge me?
I'm scared to share my dreams,
What if they tell me
To be more realistic?"
The worst part of this all,
Is that we all want the same thing!
Freedom of love,
Freedom of expression,
Authenticity
And connection.
So yes,
There is a lot
To learn from children.

"But hey,
Would you maybe
Wanna be my friend?"

Constantly escaping,
But never creating.
I wonder why I'm depressed,
They say my soul needs
Rest.
Procrastination
Or relaxation?
Do we escape
To hide our fear
Of failure?
Or is it something
So much greater?
We hide our fear
Of being too good,
Too multifaceted,
Too talented.
We're scared of our
Own light,
We shrink ourselves
To be accepted.
What's the trick to all of this?
Accept yourself,
Before anyone else
Ever could.
Delusion will always
Look crazy,
Until you make
What looks crazy,
A material and tangible
Reality.
So what reality do you want?
What does it look like?
What does it feel like?
Have that picture in your head?
Good.
Now all you have to do
Is go create it.

What are you doing here?
A vague question holding infinite avenues
Of conclusions and definitions.
Here?
In this place?
With these people?
In this world?
In this state of mind?
What are we doing here?
Is it possible,
That we're asking
questions
That were always
Meant to remain
Rhetorical?
Possibly.
What makes the human race so curious
Of our own existence?
Existential crises,
Served left and right,
Day and night.
But the moment
We see the trees,
And the birds,
And the leaves,
And the herds,
Of animals.
We realize,
They never question the
Reasons.
They realize there are seasons.
They don't know anxiety
Or depression,
They don't live in past
Or future contemplation.
They don't subscribe to the question
Of a meaningful or meaningless
Existence.

They.
Just.
Are.

The breakthrough is worth having.
It's so worth it.
The build up,
The pain,
The doubt.
It melts away
The moment you have the breakthrough.
The moment
You achieve what
You thought you couldn't do.
It's surreal,
It's shocking,
And it quite literally
Opens you up
To a new world
Of limitless opportunities.
So keep pushing.
Your breakthrough is
Always closer,
Right
When you feel most
Like giving up.

I find myself wondering about
The almost's
And the maybe's.
Sometimes,
Maybe a little too much.
Have you ever had
A piece of your favorite food
Snatched away from you?
Or lost one of your
Favorite pieces of jewelry?
Have you ever gotten
Your favorite drink
And taken a sip,
Just to realize the milk was sour?
That is how I feel about
The almosts and the maybe's.
But with people
That feeling of loss
Is far greater.
It consumes you.
It makes you wonder and
It flips your world upside down.
Making you feel like you
Know everything,
And nothing at all.
Your soul is hungry
And thirsty for their presence,
But you're stuck unable to find
Sustenance.
And in the wake
Of this thirst and hunger,
You neglect your physical
need for satiety.
Because the thing you crave
Will never come back,
You have to get used to the idea
Of new food,
New jewelry,
And an entirely new and fresh
Favorite drink.

your fellow empath

Distant,
And inconsistent.
Keep feeding me your lies
They'll be my soul's demise.
How could they call me gullible,
When the words you spoke
Were so believable?
How can I differentiate between
My heart
And my intuition?
Both seem to lead me astray
These days.
Your words say
You'll give me the world,
But your actions say
I'm just another girl,
To play with.
She's so bright,
Let me take her light,
Let me be complacent.
Please go find someone else
To fill the void within you.
You spend your days
Draining,
Chasing,
Faking,
And taking,
From others.
Until you realize
You sucked their souls
So dry,
That now your biggest
Nightmare
Has come true.
The darkest form of solitude.

You're completely,
And utterly,
Alone.

I will not let you have
Your cake and eat it too.
Not when it comes to me and you.
Your lack of accountability is something I allowed,
How stupid of me!
And no
I won't let you breadcrumb me,
When I deserve the whole fucking bakery.
But it is my fault in a sense,
Because I enabled this behavior,
And you're fine with it because you've always
Been a taker.
You build up your walls
So you won't get hurt.
Your defenses
Are knives and guns and fire
To anyone
Who tries to inspire,
The idea of loving you.
Oh you're scared?
Yeah, me too.
The difference between
Me and you,
Is I'm willing to take that risk,
Are you?
No you're not.
Have fun
Leading on
Those that toy with your emotions
because of their own fears
And traumas
Of being rejected.
I'm sick of you.
Go away.
But please come back!
Is what I pray.
You're not who you
Said you were.
You were just after
The girl next door.
And now you'll have to live
With the regret of losing her,
Forevermore.

your fellow empath

I'm sensitive.
I care.
I love deeply.
I show it.
I wear my heart on my sleeve.
I see people's power
And potential
Most times,
Surpassing levels
They could never
Comprehend
For themselves.
I push past my fears,
I say how I feel.
When others are building
Their walls,
Brick my brick
With every hurt,
And past phrase
That made them feel heartsick.
I actively break mine down
And become more aware.
I risk so much in loving others.
I push through my wounds,
My insecurities,
My fears,
To show the ones I love
That they are worth it.
They are worth facing
The darkest parts of myself.
They are worth
Facing the triggers
And the traumas.
I do this because

->

The higher the risk
The higher the reward.
Whether the output i want
Or not.
To grow in love together
Is so beautiful.
I'm trying to find people
That will match my
Willingness
To dive deeper,
But lately I've found out
How rare that is.
To face the deepest fear
Of being seen
For who we truly are,
Faults and all.
So I continue to love
Without attachment,
As hard as that is.
And I continue
To give of myself freely,
But not to those
Who don't deserve me.
Those who don't deserve me
I still love unconditionally.
But once they break
That barrier of respect
For me,
I have to love them from a distance.
Loving you
From a distance
Means maybe
There will never be a reconnection.

But don't get it twisted,
You're still forgiven.

I'm blossoming.
I love me,
I look at her
With compassion,
And I see
Her different reactions,
And I no longer
Judge her.
I know who hurt her,
And I know she deserves to
Feel hurt.
She's had her moments
Of acting out,
And she's had her moments
Of taking the higher road.
But I still love her.
She does the work,
And she no longer
Expects more.
She tries her best
And she leaves the rest.
Listening to her tired body,
Brushing her own hair,
And looking herself in the mirror
Saying,
"I'm right there."
She's gained a new perspective
and understanding of herself.
She gives to herself
What she so willingly gives
To others.
Unconditional love
And understanding.
Compassion,
Grace,
Care.
If it took all of this suffering
To get me there,

It was worth it.

“Well, how are you not scared of what people will say?”

‘That’s easy. Because in 100 years, you and I will cease to exist. And whether or not the critics like it, their dying breath will silence them and their disbelief in you. So whatever they say now, it doesn’t hold much weight. Because if I don’t go after what I was made to do, in the time allotted to me, my biological clock will run out. And I’d rather take my last dying breath full of peace knowing I fought for what I wanted, than be a naysayer and a disbeliever. But because I know this lifestyle will bring me no regrets, I pity the naysayer, because I know their regrets will haunt them.

And I wouldn’t wish that upon my worst enemy.”

Acknowledgements

I am beyond thankful to be in a time here on earth that self publishing my art and having a platform to reach anyone from the world is a possibility. I'd like to acknowledge my incredible family and friends, for pushing me to pursue my art and creative endeavors. If you're reading this, you know who you are. Thank you for texting me, calling me, and sending me messages of inspiration to keep pushing and never give up. Your words of encouragement go farther than you could ever imagine.

Secondly, I would like to thank myself. I started writing poetry when other forms of art were not a possibility for me. I was able to express myself silently, in a time of my life that I felt completely hopeless. To transmute the pain I never thought I would heal through, into something that has blessed my life is something I never thought I'd be able to do.

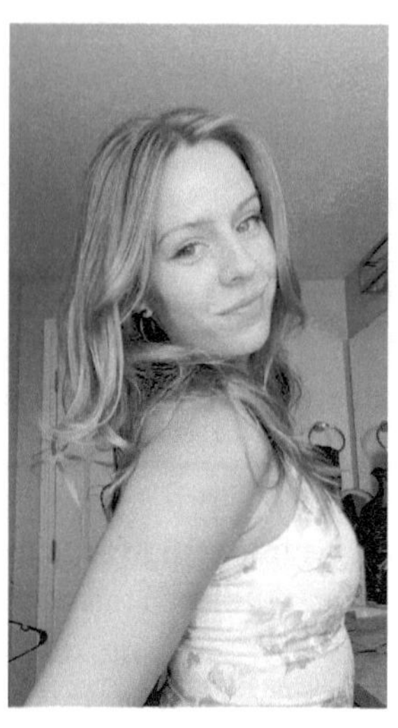

About the Author

Kenzie Chapman is an Entrepreneur and first-time Author from Ogden Utah. She is passionate about art in many forms including dancing, singing, and of course, poetry. When not writing poetry, you can find her having multiple identity crises and dreaming of leaving everything and everyone behind to escape to beautiful beaches around the world.

Find more of their work:
Instagram:
@kenz_chap

Work by McKenzie Chapman

Your Fellow Empath

Available on Amazon and wherever fine books are sold

www.ingramcontent.com/pod-product-compliance
Lightning Source LLC
LaVergne TN
LVHW090534110826
845146LV00003B/1096

9798991176101